Focus on Feelings

© Play Therapy with Carmen

Positive and Negative Cognitions

Carmen Jimenez-Pride

MSW, LCSW, LISW-CP, SAP, RYT, RCYT, RPT-S

ABOUT THE AUTHOR

Carmen Jimenez-Pride, creator of Focus on Feelings® is a Licensed Clinical Social Worker and Registered Play Therapist Supervisor, Certified EMDR Therapist, Certified Internal Family Systems Therapist. She is an international speaker, awarded winning best-selling author and business consultant.

Carmen Jimenez-Pride is also the founder of Diversity in Play Therapy Inc. and the host of the Diversity in Play Therapy Summit.

Contact: **www.carmenpride.com**

Email: **Carmen@outspokenllc.com**

ABOUT THIS BOOK

This Focus on Feelings® resource is intended for use by EMDR trained therapists with clients to assist with EMDR therapy.

This book coordinates with the Focus on Feelings® Cognitions Card Deck and Focus on Feelings® Scale Dial.

This resource can also be used within other therapeutic models for both children and adults!

I can protect myself !

I can not protect myself.

I am safe !

I am not safe.

I am important !

I am not important.

I am okay just like I am !

There is something wrong with me.

I did the best I could !

I should have done something.

I am good !

I am bad.

I belong.

I do not belong.

I can show my feelings.

I can not show my feelings.

The way I feel is okay.

The way I feel
is not okay.

Others can help me get what I need !

I have to get what I need.

I can choose who to trust.

I can not trust anyone.

I am loveable.

I am not loveable.

I deserve to be loved.

I do not deserve
to be loved.

I can get help.

I can not get help.

I am strong.

I am weak.

I can make it through this.

I can not make
it through this.

I am smart.

I am stupid.

It is not my fault.

It is my fault.

I can do many things.

I can not do things.

I can be happy.

I can not be happy !

There are many good things about me.

There is nothing good about me.

I like the way I look !

I do not like the way I look.

I am good enough !

I am not good enough.

I deserve to have food !

I do not deserve food.

It is not my responsibility.

I should have
done something.

I can relax.

I can not relax.